SUPER
WOMAN
SMARTS

WORKBOOK

No part of this book may be reproduced, stored in a retrieval system or transmitted in any form or by any means without the prior written permission of the publishers, except by a reviewer who may quote brief passages in a review to be printed in a newspaper, magazine or journal.

SUPERWOMAN SMARTS: 21-Day Brand Boot Camp Workbook

Herein, I have developed a series of maneuvers, including online and offline strategies that will not only re-energize YOU, they will help you makeover your existing brand, regardless of the perception you currently have, or where you are in your career lifecycle. This program is only intended to jump start, or 'boost' your brand campaign. Future branding activities should depend on what you learn about your brand as you execute this starter sequence.

Reputation:

It can mean the difference between professional success and complacency. Yes, it matters what other people think of you—whether you agree or approve of what they're saying or not. Your personal brand is what people say about you, or think about you when you are not in the room. In other words, it's what people say about you behind your back. Do you know what the public is saying? Like it or not, their perception is your reality. What do you want them to say about you? What is the brand that you aspire to have?

Obviously, you don't have 100% control of your brand, but you can manipulate it—and you certainly should try. If you don't control your brand or manage your reputation, someone else will do it for you. Brand is created over time, and it can be measured. There are many metrics for tracking brand reputation available today, and some are more vital and meaningful than others. You know as well as I do that when we measure or track something, it usually improves. Similar to keeping a food journal or weighing yourself each morning, you should be tracking your personal brand systematically.

DAY ONE

DEFINE YOUR BRAND

Define the words and phrases that describe you. What do you stand for? What's your label? What do people say about YOU? Use listening tools to hear what people are saying about you, for example, Google Alerts, TweetDeck, and RSS feeds.

Now, write down what you *want* them to say about you. What is the brand that you want to be known for? What keywords and phrases do you want to be associated with you? How will you make people believe this brand is representative of you?

_____

_____

_____

_____

_____

_____

_____

_____

_____

_____

DAY TWO

FIND A MENTOR

Remember that he or she who has achieved success has had help and support along the way. Some of the big heads out there may not acknowledge it, but everyone needs someone. Real success is a shared experience.

Often, people say they want a mentor, but they are not ready to listen yet. They say they want help, but they are still inflexible and a know-it-all. They want to talk, not listen; they want to do, not learn. Isn't it strange how we don't listen to the ones around us that love us, but we listen to others who are complete strangers?

_____

_____

_____

_____

_____

_____

_____

_____

_____

_____

DAY THREE

RESERVE YOUR PERSONAL DOMAIN NAME

Do you own your own personal domain name? You should. And while you're at it, reserve domains for your children who will thank you later. This is one clear way to create your own brand real estate. And don't just own your own domain, use it. Create your own fresh content. Send new contacts to your web site where they can learn more about you, and also immediately get something of value from you. Giveaway a newsletter, report, brochure, publication, infographic, poster, or sample.

_____

_____

_____

_____

_____

_____

_____

_____

_____

_____

_____

DAY FOUR

GO PUBLIC

When something good happens to you, get the word out immediately. Let your colleagues and the community know that you have reached an important milestone. If possible, get someone else to help tell your story, for example, TV, radio, or a newspaper interview. In particular, women don't promote themselves, even when they should. Whether you like to do it or not, it's good for business and branding, when it's done the right way. Women who say they don't like to promote themselves secretly wish that someone else would do it for them. If you know someone like this, help them get their story out.

_____

_____

_____

_____

_____

_____

_____

_____

_____

DAY FIVE

SAY "YES" (SELECTIVELY)

I truly believe everyone should bite off a little more than they can chew. Don't be as afraid of success, as you are of failure. Have the courage to say "Yes" to the right things—things you are passionate about and that align with your purpose. If you feel like you don't have the opportunity at work to do more, you can volun-CHEER!

Inquire at your local Chamber of Commerce about opportunities to volunteer.

_____

_____

_____

_____

_____

_____

_____

_____

_____

_____

DAY SIX

SUBMIT AN ARTICLE

Submit an article to a magazine or journal, or ask to write a guest blog post for your favorite web site. It's true, old-fashioned writing is a great way to build authority in your niche. If you decide to do it, follow the established guidelines and meet the agreed upon submission target date.

Quora is a great source of topics to write about. Quora is a Q&A website where users pose questions and other users answer them.

_____

_____

_____

_____

_____

_____

_____

_____

_____

_____

DAY SEVEN

GET LINKEDIN

LinkedIn is your professional resume to the world, so make sure your profile is complete including geography, number of years of experience, degree qualifications, etc. Don't over rely on past achievements. What have you done lately? Your profile should show continued progress and growth.

Add as much relevant detail as needed.

_____
_____
_____
_____
_____
_____
_____
_____
_____
_____

DAY EIGHT

CONTINUE TO LEARN

Smart people always have something to share. Read a book or subscribe to a leading industry publication. Or, take a class and attend a national conference at least once annually. This is a great way to meet a lot of new people and impress them with your depth and breadth of knowledge and abilities.

_____

_____

_____

_____

_____

_____

_____

_____

_____

DAY NINE

WRITE A THANK YOU CARD

You may be thinking that Thank You cards are outdated, but the truth is we still smile when we get a handwritten note from someone in the mail, don't we? A handwritten note is more personal and shows you care enough to give a little extra effort.

_____

_____

_____

_____

_____

_____

_____

_____

_____

DAY TEN

FAIL FORWARD

Be UNFLAPPABLE—persistently calm, whether when facing difficulties or experiencing success; not easily upset or excited. Learn from your mistakes and move on quickly without a lot of self-criticism or self-pity. Remember, if you're not failing you're not growing.

_____

_____

_____

_____

_____

_____

_____

_____

_____

_____

DAY ELEVEN

SEARCH YOUR NAME ON GOOGLE

Have you ever searched for your own name on Google? As much as possible, people need to control their online search results, because they frequently contain inaccurate, misleading or outdated material which can adversely influence how web searchers view them. When you type your name in the Google search box, the returned results should be primarily content that you have populated online yourself.

_____

_____

_____

_____

_____

_____

_____

_____

_____

_____

DAY TWELVE

CLEAN HOUSE

There are many brand killers. Not practicing what you preach is a top destroyer of brands. Being caught publicly doing something inappropriate, especially if you have role model status—or aspire to—is the number one killer. Take down inappropriate pictures and comments that you may have posted when you were not in your right mind. It's true that once it's out there, it's out there. But, would you never clean your house again, because you knew it was just going to get dirty again? At the very least, clean up your own house. Try to keep it clean from here on out.

_____

_____

_____

_____

_____

_____

_____

_____

_____

_____

DAY THIRTEEN

SECURE YOUR BRAND ON THE INTERNET

Resistance to social media is futile. Millions of people are creating content for the social web; your competitors are already there; your customers and colleagues have been there for a long time; if you aren't already putting yourself out there, you should be. Social media play time is OVER … so get SERIOUS about harnessing the power of this thing!

_____

_____

_____

_____

_____

_____

_____

_____

_____

_____

DAY FOURTEEN

GET HELP IF YOU NEED IT

Ask around if you don't know where to begin. There are countless life coaches and counselors who provide image consulting. I am a stickler about selecting people to work with who set records and examples in their industry. How can they help you with brand, if they don't have one? If you hire a life coach, they better have a colorful story to tell about their own life and challenges they have overcome.

_____

_____

_____

_____

_____

_____

_____

_____

DAY FIFTEEN

SYNCHRONIZE YOUR SOCIAL AND OFFLINE PRESENCE

Create a CONSISTENT brand identity across all marketing channels. For instance, use the same picture on all of your profiles to maximize your branding efforts. Subsequently, when others encounter your brand, they will recognize it immediately. They don't have to wonder, "Is that her?" Consistency and frequency are key to creating a memorable brand. As tempting as it may be, don't change your photo/brand identity often. Your printed material, web site, and advertising should look like it belongs to the same family. If everything looks different, your brand is going to be weak, diluted and indistinguishable.

_____

_____

_____

_____

_____

_____

_____

_____

_____

_____

DAY SIXTEEN

MEASURE YOUR SOCIAL REPUTATION

Measure your audience, engagement, loyalty, influence, and action. Yes, you can measure these indicators for your brand. Tools like *Brandify* and *Naymz* can be used to measure and manage your reputation. I like these products, because they not only tell you how you are doing, they provide suggestions for raising your score.

_____

_____

_____

_____

_____

_____

_____

_____

_____

_____

DAY SEVENTEEN

ASK FOR AN ENDORSEMENT

Ask for testimonials and feedback–build relationships. The best time to ask for an endorsement is when you've just completed a successful project or initiative. Don't wait until you are without a job to ask for a letter of reference or commendation. Your professional portfolio should be current at all times. Give endorsements as well; nobody likes a taker—only looking for what's in it for them.

_____

_____

_____

_____

_____

_____

_____

_____

_____

_____

DAY EIGHTEEN

ANSWER A QUESTION

Many times, on social media channels, people are too self-serving; it's always about them and their projects. Not giving enough back to your contact network is a no-no. Take the time to answer business-related questions posted by peers. Offer to help solve a problem. Provide a referral or recommend a connection. In your response, refer to a document, recent report or case study to back up your comments. When you answer questions, you increase your credibility and authority in your industry.

_____

_____

_____

_____

_____

_____

_____

_____

_____

_____

DAY NINETEEN

GET ACTIVE

Don't feel as though you have to be active on all social channels, but update your social status regularly for 1-2 primary accounts. Don't make people wonder what happened to you. Make thoughtful comments. Be RESPONSIVE. Engage. Be conversational.

Create a distinct strategy for each social channel rather than update in rapid-fire style, but don't be afraid to post some of the same information on multiple networks if it's appropriate.

_____

_____

_____

_____

_____

_____

_____

_____

_____

_____

_____

DAY TWENTY

LEAVE TOWN

Have you ever heard of the 300-Mile Rule? I have found that when I travel to speak to groups I actually get a little more audience love and appreciation. When you are the visitor, the audience recognizes the fact that you had to get up early that day and get in your car, to drive in to see them—that it was worth your time to do so. On the other hand, sometimes the people you work with everyday forget how fantastic you are—especially if you are a regular high-performer. At home, the WOW factor can wear off, frankly. Consequently, don't stop WOWing, but consider taking your WOW on a vacation, and let it out for a run once in a while to keep it in shape.

_____

_____

_____

_____

_____

_____

_____

_____

_____

_____

DAY TWENTY-ONE

BE MEMORABLE

Your Unique Selling Proposition is what sets you apart and makes you truly different from others. I have a colleague who I have noticed lately wearing a bright colored neck scarf, as part of her daily wardrobe. This is how she has chosen to stand out in a room full of people. Another woman that I know is always wearing an extraordinary pair of heels with bling even in the most conservative setting.

_____

_____

_____

_____

_____

_____

_____

_____

_____

_____

_____

_____

_____

_____

_____

_____

_____

_____

_____

_____

_____

QUESTIONS? COMMENTS? CONTACT ME?

Aundrea Wilcox, President

Intrepid Business Strategies

1657B E Stone Dr. Ste. 196

Kingsport, TN 37660-4609

United States

Toll Free: (800) 560-1387

Fax: (800) 560-1387

Web Site: intrepidbizstrategies.com

Email: awilcox@intrepidbizstrategies.com

AUNDREA Y. WILCOX, Brenau University MBA, is currently the Senior Business Counselor of the Tennessee Small Business Development Center (TSBDC) at East Tennessee State University (ETSU) Kingsport Affiliate Office, and Executive Director of the Kingsport Office of Small Business Development & Entrepreneurship (KOSBE) at the Kingsport Area Chamber of Commerce, Tenn. She has provided technical assistance to over 1,200 individuals or businesses.

Previously, Aundrea provided expert testimony at a hearing of the Subcommittee on Contracting and Technology of the U.S. House of Representatives Committee on Small Business in Washington, D.C., and served as a session moderator on "Small Business Incubation" at the 55th Annual Tennessee Governor's Conference on Economic & Community Development.

In addition to being a full-time GrowthWheel Certified Business Advisor™, Aundrea has a long tradition of community service. She currently serves on the Holston Valley Medical Center Board of Directors as a member of the Executive Committee and Co-Chair of the Joint Quality Committee; she is a Board Member of the Holston Business Development Center Small Business Incubator; and a past member of the Board of Directors of the Northeast Tennessee Regional Entrepreneurial Accelerator. She is also a Selection Committee Member for the East Tennessee State University Roan Scholars Leadership Program.

Aundrea Y. Wilcox is also the author of *Startup Savvy: Strategies for Optimizing Small Business Survival and Success*; and a contributing blogger on business and finance to The BOSS Network, which was recently named by Forbes.com as one of the Top 10 Entrepreneurial Websites for Women, and one of the Top 10 Best Career Sites for Women. She also recently collaborated with 25 consultants affiliated with the U.S. Small Business Development Center (SBDC) program, to help write a new book, The TriStart™ Matrix, which is designed to help entrepreneurs master three critical phases for a successful business start.

Originally from Michigan, Aundrea resides in Kingsport, Tennessee, with her husband Lonnie L. Salyer, a graduate of the University of Tennessee, who also earned his MBA from East Tennessee State University, and is currently a Global Procurement Manager of Energy at Eastman Chemical Company. Between them, they have two children—Barbara (21) and Cody (15).

Startup Savvy:
Strategies for Optimizing Small Business Survival and Success

ISBN-13: 978-1456097479
ISBN-10: 1456097474

Startup Savvy is jam-packed with relatable real-world entrepreneurial stories combined with rock solid advice to help you optimize your small business success!

Superwoman Smarts:
Activating Leadership & Substance

ISBN-13: 978-1503032866
ISBN-10: 1503032868

Superwoman Smarts is all about women, but smart men will read it too—for a better understanding of the women in their life. It's about learning from each other, embracing each other, accepting our differences and achieving success, and doing more with what we have.